NO PHONES IN HEAVEN

By
Lisa Ann

Sal,
May life give you
all the blessings you
truly deserve! ☺
Peace Love & Light
Lisa Ann

A Spiritquest Productions Publication

P.O. Box 174
Slate Hill, NY 10973
(845) 355-8022
lisaann@spiritquesthealingcenter.com

ISBN:
978-0-9794596-0-3

Also By Lisa Ann

Angelic Whispers
Guided Meditation CD

Body Mind Spirit
Guided Meditation CD

Dedication

This book is dedicated to:

My beloved Grandma Jennie, whose death started me on my psychic journey.

My Grandfather, fondly known as "Papa" Sam, whose illness and ultimate death started my journey of becoming a healer.

My mother who taught me women can do anything men can do.

My father who taught me you learn a lot more by being quiet.

My two beautiful children, Anthony and Jenna, it is because of the two of you that I never gave up!

Anthony, I watch you fearlessly time after time racing around the track. You have taught me and inspired me to have that same fearless attitude about life! Your driving skills will take you far but your attitude will take you even farther!

Jenna, you are not only my daughter but my teacher. Your love of life and uncanny ability to manifest everything you desire into your life is not only inspiring but contagious! Keep Dreaming! Keep Believing! Keep Surfing!

I would like to thank my best friend, Ann Bell, for her continued support, belief in me, and most of all, for never allowing me to give up!

Thank you all!

Special Thanks

I would like to thank Sarahanne Blake for her help in editing this book and for all of her wonderful insights and suggestions.

I would like to thank Linda Zimmermann, ghost investigator and author, for all of her support, encouragement, and help in publishing this book.

I also want to thank James Riley "Rye". He is without a doubt one of the most talented and artistic people I know. He has an uncanny ability to take the visions in my head and effortlessly make them a reality! He created the music for my CD (Body, Mind and Spirit) as well as doing all of the art work on both CD's (Body, Mind and Spirit & Angelic Whispers). His dedication and commitment in designing the cover and doing all the art work on this book was more than I could have ever expected. Thank you!

Most of all, I want to thank the thousands of clients I have seen over the years for their continued support and love. Each one of them has touched my life; we have laughed and cried together. It is because of all of you that I continue to do what I do!

CONTENTS

Introduction   7

Chapter 1   Dream Visions   11

Chapter 2   Please Help Me   17

Chapter 3   The Converted Atheist   23

Chapter 4   The Boy and the Motorcycle   27

Chapter 5   The Gold Rose   37

Chapter 6   Duckie, Duckie, Duckie   41

Chapter 7   Grandma Jennie Saves the Day   45

Chapter 8   To Stay or to Go   57

Chapter 9   Sept 11th - A Son's Message to His Dad   65

Chapter 10   The Meucci Haunting–Re-writing History   73

Chapter 11   A Teacher from the Other Side   93

Chapter 12   Death & Dying   99

About Lisa Ann   108

Introduction

The veil between the world of the living and the world of the dead is a lot thinner than most people think. There are spirits all around us, and as you will see through the stories in this book, they are very willing and able to communicate with us. We simply need to listen.

We are constantly hearing references to the "Other Side" but where is the "Other Side?" It is my belief system that the "Other Side" isn't this place way up high; I believe it exists in the same space that we do. I believe that our loved ones are right around us! So next time you are longing to connect with a loved one who has passed, don't look up; look right besides you!

The stories in this book are just some of the experiences I have had throughout my many years of communicating with literally thousands of spirits who have passed. The stories are sad, shocking, life altering, but always inspirational. They remind us that life is something to be cherished everyday. They remind us that our loved ones are never far away. They remind us to always tell the people in our lives that we love them!

Please be aware that some of the names have been changed, or the last names omitted where necessary, to protect the privacy of my clients.

Do we see with our eyes or our minds?

Dream Visions

When I was around 12 years old my parents were in the process of having a new home built. We had visited the house earlier that day to check on how things were coming along. My parents were very excited because all of the appliances had just been delivered, which meant moving day was right around the corner. While inspecting the house, my parents were very upset to find out that the vent in the laundry room had not yet been installed, which meant that anyone could easily crawl in through the opening and get into the house. My parents were concerned especially since all their new appliances had just been delivered. That night I would have my very first "dream vision."

My parents had two good friends that lived in the development where the house was being built. One family had three children and the other family had four. We had known them for many years and all of us kids used to hang out together, the age ranges were from 4 to 15. In my dream it was nighttime and I was walking up the road to the new house. I was with all of the kids and their parents', however my parents' were not there. As we got up to the house, the oldest boy and myself climbed in through the open missing vent. He climbed in first and I followed. He had a flashlight in his hand and he guided the way through the dark house to the front door. He then opened the front door and let everyone else in. And the dream ended.

The thing that made this dream different from any other dream I had ever had was that I could feel the chill of the night. The older boy that I climbed through the window with had hit his teenage years and had recently discovered cologne. Unfortunately, no one told him not to wear the entire bottle, so you could literally smell him coming before you could see him. In my dream I could smell his cologne as well as the construction smell of a new house. Everything was so real. It was unlike anything I had ever experienced in my life.

When I woke up that morning the dream was fresh on my mind and I went down to tell my mother all about it. I remember that I kept saying that it was like I was there. It was so real!

A few hours later, one of my mom's friends from the development called. She was the mother of the boy who I climbed through the window with in my dream. She was calling to tell my mom that they had been sitting outside the night before with the other family that we knew when they noticed a truck with no license plates go up the street to our new house. They were concerned because they never saw it come back down. She informed my mom that they all took a walk up to the house and the oldest boy climbed in through the open vent, went to the front door, and let them all in. She informed my mom that they had checked the entire house and everything looked fine and luckily all the appliances were there.

I could not believe my ears when my mother told me the story. Could it be? Was I actually there with them? Was it one of those psychic premonitions or was I actually experiencing all the events at the same time? Had I astral traveled (when your body is in one place but your spirit is in another)?

I never really thought anything more about it till years later as my reputation and success as a psychic began to unfold. People constantly started asking me when I knew I had the "gift." To this day I insist it is not a gift, but rather a sense that we all have and one that we can easily tap into. However, the constant questions lead me to really take some time to think back to my childhood. As I skimmed through my memory, I realized I did indeed have several scattered experiences as a child.

It is my belief that we are all psychic, or, as I prefer to call it, intuitive. Whenever I teach or lecture I always tell people that I am NOT going to teach them how to become psychic. I am going to teach them how to become psychically aware.

Dreams are very important and can be useful when seeking direction in your life. Everyone dreams, everyone can train himself or herself to remember their dreams. The best way to begin to train yourself to remember your dreams is to start by keeping a note pad and pen by your bed. As soon as you wake up write down whatever you can remember. The more you practice the more you will begin to remember. There are no short cuts to remembering your dreams. Some people suggest that you drink a lot of water before bed so you will wake up in the middle of the night to go to the bathroom, therefore interrupting the dream. When you awake, the dream will be fresh in your mind.

Now here is where I get myself in trouble. There are a million dream interpretation books, dream interpretation specialist, and so on. It has always been my philosophy that the best way to make sense of your dreams is to not look to others or to the books, but instead, look for what symbols, people, or things stood out the most. Think about what those symbols, people, or things mean to you. Keep track of your dreams and look for reoccurring themes. Before you know it, you will become your own dream interpretation expert!

Do we speak with our words or our thoughts?

Please Help Me

When I was about 18 I had a very disturbing dream that literally took me years to figure out. In my dream I was sitting on a couch with my grandfather who was still alive and well. There was a dead body lying across us under a sheet. My grandfather and I were discussing how sad it was that grandma had died. Now, in the dream I was very well aware of the fact that it was not my grandmother under the sheet since she was alive and well at the time. As we continued discussing the sadness of her passing, the women under the sheet sat straight up and grabbed me by my shirt! She kept yelling at me, "Please help me, you have to help me!" I remember yelling back at her in the dream that I couldn't help her because she was dead. I am not sure how long this went on but it seemed like an eternity. I woke up after the dream and was terrified! I eventually fell back to sleep and woke up the next morning with no memory of the dream.

It wouldn't be until later on that day when I was getting ready to go out that the dream would come screaming back to me. It was nightfall by this time; I walked into my room and flipped the light switch on. As soon as the brightness of the light hit my eyes the dream came flooding back into my memory. I don't know why, but I had absolutely no memory of the dream the entire day. Needless to say, I was extremely shaken up. I was so upset that, at 18, I was afraid to sleep by myself that night.

The next morning or the morning after, our neighbor called, by this time we were living happily in our new development, the two families I previously mentioned (see Dream Vision story) and my family had become very close. The neighbor was calling to tell my parents' that her mom had been killed the night before in a horrible accident. Her mom was on vacation in Florida and was crossing a street when a tractor-trailer went by, apparently the suction of the passing truck pulled her into the road and she was killed.

I couldn't believe it when my mother told me. It all made sense now. The dream, the death, the plea for help, she didn't want to die, or so I thought. And now, even the part about me calling her grandma in the dream made sense. I had grown up with this family and we all called each other's grandparents' grandma and grandpa like they were our own. I felt horrible for being unable to help her; I wondered what I could have done.

This dream continued to haunt me. I began feeling like it was my job to let our neighbor know that her mom didn't want to die. One day I decided to go and talk with her. As we began to talk about our belief systems and life after death she began to tell me how even though it was a horrible and tragic event, she somehow felt her mother's spirit knew she was going to be passing. She told me that when they cleaned out the mother's apartment they had found Christmas presents for everyone, wrapped and labeled. She found this extremely odd because her mother apparently was one of those last minute shoppers that would always call a few days before Christmas asking for a ride to the store so she could buy gifts for all the kids and grandkids. Now you may be thinking, so the woman shopped early, but she died in May! Another weird occurrence was that she had apparently mailed a birthday card to her granddaughter, which arrived several weeks later on her birthday!

At this point I felt more lost then ever. I thought for sure the grandmother was telling me she didn't want to die. I thought for sure that her pleas for help were for me to somehow save her! I never did tell her daughter what I thought because she had such a sense of peace believing that somehow her mother's spirit had known of what was to come. It wasn't until many years later that I would fully understand this dream.

I was teaching a class one day when once again the discussion of when I knew I had a gift came up. As I was reminiscing about my earlier dreams and experiences, I shared the story of the woman under the sheet. Next, someone asked me when was the first time I knew I could communicate with the dead, which as a medium (a person who communicates with spirits and people who have passed), I get a lot. I don't know why I had never connected it in all those years, but there was something about the two questions being asked one right after another that struck me like a bolt of lightning and in that split second it all made sense. The woman below the sheet was not asking me to save her; she was asking me "to help her" and to get a message to her family! Of course, at 18 I didn't know how to communicate with the dead, I didn't even know it was possible! I felt such a sense of relief after having my new understanding of the dream and what she was trying to tell me. I also had a new understanding of how the spirit sometimes prepares us for things we don't even realize are about to happen on the human level.

What you believe today, you may not believe tomorrow.

The Converted Atheist

I had just started reading tarot cards for friends and family when a co-worker from my regular job called me one night in a panic. She wanted to know if I could do a reading for her but she didn't want me to know why or have me ask her any questions, as her dilemma was a very private matter. I had worked with Susan for several months and would consider her more an acquaintance then a friend. She was one of those people that really never said anything about anything and there wasn't much about her that I knew, except that she was married, was in her late 40's, had no children, and didn't believe in much, especially not God. You could imagine my shock when she called with her reading request.

It was late and everyone in my house was asleep. So I quietly went into the dining room and began to spread out my cards. As I began looking over the cards I got an image of a woman in my head. I heard her say that her name was Edith. I was a little startled, especially since I was sitting in the dark by myself. I honestly thought I was going nuts when I unknowingly blurted out, "Do you know an older woman named Edith?" Susan burst out crying and said, "That was my grandmother! How could you possibly know that? She has been dead for years!" WHAT! She thought she was shocked; I was speechless!

Apparently the spirit world, being all knowing, wasn't really too concerned with the breakdown I was about to have since the woman, Edith, just continued talking. She went on to tell me that she loved the new wallpaper that Susan had recently put up in her bathroom and described the wallpaper in detail. She continued on telling me how she and Susan shared a love of antiques. She told me how just recently, Susan was in an Antique shop and saw a lamp that reminded her of her grandmother. Her grandmother joked that Susan was usually very money conscious (cheap) but that she just bought this lamp with out even looking at the price.

Of course, Susan was able to confirm everything her grandmother had told me. But as shocking as this all was, the grandmother was not done yet! I was told to look at certain cards as the grandmother continued to fill in a shocking story. Apparently Susan did have a child. She had a child out of wedlock many years ago! Her husband didn't even know! Another family member had been raising the son all these years as their own and now there was some talk of them reuniting. Needless to say, this was a shocking experience for the both of us. I am not sure whatever happened after that as we went our separate ways in the job and I never saw her again. I do know she had a new belief in the afterlife and in God!

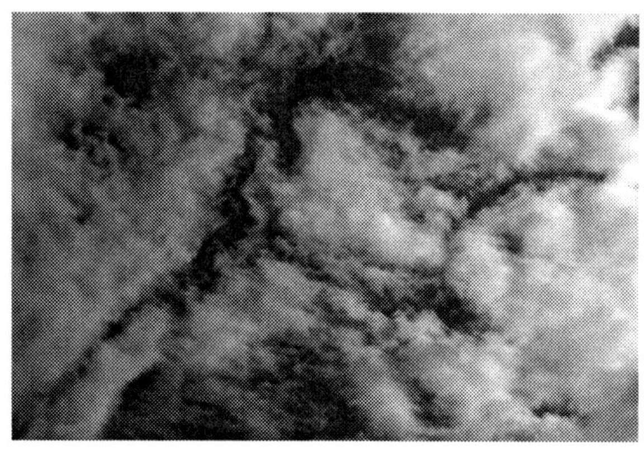

The love between a child and parent is like no other.

The Boy and the Motor cycle

I was at a party for a child of a friend of mine when someone came up to me and said, "Did you hear what happened last night?" They went on to inform me that a young man in our development had been killed in a motorcycle accident the night before. It is always traumatic to hear of someone so young taken so early. Jim was only in his early 20's. I didn't know him personally, but I did know the family through a business they owned and because my sister went to school with his sister.

By this time I had been reading for a couple of years and I had done many readings connecting people with loved ones who had passed, so I was a little more comfortable with the process. The next day I was driving down the road, radio blasting, singing to a great song when I heard very loud and strong, "You need to help me, you need to tell my mother it wasn't my fault." At the same time I heard the words, I saw an image in my head. It was like I was transported in time and I was on a motorcycle. I could see my hand on the throttle going back and forth. I felt myself look down and then look up. I felt the panic overcome me as I realized I was going off the road. The voice continued, "You have to tell her it wasn't my fault."

My first reaction was that I was just imagining all of this. I just thought that I was letting my fear and reality of this tragedy play with my head. As the mother of two children, one boy and one girl, it was very easy to connect with the horror of having to bury one of your children because of such an awful accident.

A few days later I was in our local deli. The accident had been the talk of our little town. A man standing in front of me was talking to the deli owner who was behind the counter and of course they were discussing the accident. The deli owner made a comment on how horrible it was and how bad he felt for the family. The idiot standing in front of me (and trust me, I am being very nice in only using the word "idiot") replied by saying that he didn't feel sorry for the "stupid" kid who was driving like a maniac, he felt sorry for the poor person that found him! I IMMEDIATELY heard the voice again, "Do you hear what they are saying about me? It wasn't my fault, it was the bike!" I wasn't sure if I was more shocked by the voice or by the stupidity of the man in the deli. The voice probably saved me from being arrested that day because I honestly wanted nothing more than to slap the man in the face. But of course, that probably wouldn't have been very spiritual of me.

The voice continued for the next several days. The request was always the same, to please go and talk to his mother. By this time I had accepted that if I wasn't insane, this spirit was not going to leave me alone, so I started to converse with him. I told him that I was NOT going to just show up at his mother's door and say, "Hey listen I talk to the dead and your son has a message." I tried to convince him that he needed to get someone else. But he persisted. Then I told him I needed some kind of proof to prove to myself that I was indeed speaking to him. He told me that his grandfather met him on the other side. He told me that the accident wasn't his fault and that he wasn't speeding. He told me to please tell his girlfriend that he loved her and that this time he was going to marry her. He also showed me a dresser. It was a low, eight drawer dresser and he opened the top drawer on the right side and told me that there was something in there he wanted his girlfriend to have. I just made mental notes of all the information as I pondered what the heck to do with it all. After all, I was still getting used to the whole idea of talking to the dead; how was I going to explain it to someone else?

One morning I was in the shower when I heard the voice again. Something was different this time. There was an urgency that I hadn't heard before. He was begging me to go and talk to his mom and he said I had to do it that morning. By now these little conversations were becoming a daily event and I began conversing with him like you would any other person, any other living person that is. As ridiculous as it sounds, I nicely explained to him that I was very busy and I didn't have time.
He insisted I had to go there but I had a very busy day ahead and much to his frustration I was not able or willing to follow through

on his request. I was on my way to a local angel shop where I was doing readings a few times a week. On the way I decided to pass by his parents' house. As I drove by I noticed quite a large number of cars parked in front. There was NO WAY I was stopping!

I got to the angel shop about 15 minutes later. I had called the shop before I left and the owner confirmed with me that I had 4 or 5 appointments that I was very excited about. I parked in front of the shop, tarot cards in hand, and eagerly went in wondering what would unfold in the upcoming readings. As I walked through the door there stood the owner with a very perplexed look on her face. I didn't even get out a hello when she said, "You are not going to believe this, but ALL of your readings cancelled in the last few minutes! I don't understand it because I had confirmed all of them and they weren't even people that knew each other and they weren't even coming together!" Well that was disappointing. I was so aggravated I got up early for nothing, as I am NOT a morning person.

I got in my car and as I went to start it I heard the voice again, "There, now you are not busy, now will you go to see my mother?" I cannot tell you the shock that overcame me. I drove as fast as I could to my parents' house. And I have to tell you as I drove by the local mental hospital I seriously wondered if it was not nearing time for me to check myself in. Could it be that this spirit was behind my appointments canceling?

I walked into to my parents' house and as I walked in the kitchen my mother took one look at me and said, "What is wrong with you? You look like you saw a ghost." If she only knew! I began divulging the entire story explaining that while I had not seen a ghost I was definitely being haunted by one. I then asked my mother if she had the papers from that week, as I wanted to look up the obituary and see if the grandfather was listed as a surviving relative. I figured if he wasn't listed then I would know that it was possible that his grandfather had indeed met him on the other side, which of course would mean that all of the other information was true. That is how I looked at it, anyway. Bingo, the grandfather had passed, and after speaking with my mother, we decided it was indeed time to pay the mother of this boy a visit.

I cannot explain the absolute panic I was in while driving over there. I had no idea what I was going to say or how I would be received. The entire time I just kept telling him that I did not want to knock on the door. I kept telling him to please have his mother outside. As we pulled up on the driveway I could not believe my eyes! There was his mother on the front lawn watering the flowers. I went into a panic and I am sure if you looked, you could see my heart pounding right through my shirt. To this day I don't even remember how the conversation started, as I was scared to death!

I think my mother started by offering her condolences and telling her that her dad (my grandfather) had just passed and how she couldn't imagine losing a child. It was then that I stepped forward.

I started by telling her how hard it was for me to be there and I needed her to know that before I told her what I needed to say. I began by telling her that I didn't know what her belief system was but that I had this ability to talk to people who had passed and that her son had a message for her. I began to tell her how he wanted her to know that he loved her and that the accident wasn't his fault. I went on about the dresser and the information for the girlfriend. I told her that he was okay and how he told me that his grandfather met him on the other side. I was in mid–sentence, shaking as I continued to speak, when she freaked out. She began yelling at me, telling me to get off her property and asking me what kind of person was I and how could I do this to her. I am sure she even threatened to call the police. I panicked and started apologizing profusely as I began backing up, assuring her I was leaving. Then I heard the voice again, "Tell her it was okay that she wasn't there, tell her it was okay; I didn't want her to see me like that." Was this boy out of his mind? Was he trying to land me in prison? As I continued backing my way to the car I spoke again. "I am leaving," I promised her, "But he wants me to tell you that it was okay you weren't there, he didn't want you to see him like that, his grandfather helped him pass, it was okay." She immediately stopped yelling at me, came over, hugged me and began to cry. "How could you know that?"

She went on to tell me the entire horrible story. Apparently he had just gotten the motorcycle a day or two before and was going out for a ride. She was out watering the front lawn when she was overcome with a horrible feeling that something bad had happened to her son. She immediately got in the car and began driving down the road where she happened upon and accident. She instantly got out of the car and ran over to the officer on site. "Is there a motorcycle involved? I think it is my son? Is it my son?" she said. The officer would not let her through and instead she was detoured and returned home. As she pulled into her driveway the police pulled in behind her and informed her that her son was dead. The guilt that this woman felt in not being there when her son took his last breathe was unlike anything I had ever felt. I kept reassuring her that her son did not want her there. I assured her that he did not want her to remember him like that.

As we continued speaking, a car pulled up the driveway. She became very upset and asked my mother to get rid of whoever it was. As she turned to make her way to the house she tripped over the garden hose. It was very apparent that she was heavily medicated and I thought the least I could do was to help her to the house. I opened the door and helped her in again telling her how sorry I was and how it was not my intention to upset her. She insisted I come in and told me she had something to show me.

I followed her into the house and down the hall. As I turned to enter her bedroom I noticed a dresser with a large number of prescription bottles on it. I heard the voice again, "Now do you understand why you are here?" I replied with a simple, "Yes I do and I promise you I will take care of it." She was taking me in her room to let me look out her bedroom window so I could see her son's dog, but I was able to see the dog from outside where we were standing, so there was really no reason for me to enter the home.
It became very apparent to me that my job was not yet finished. I asked a nephew that was staying with her if I could have a word

with him. I asked him about all the medicine on the dresser and he explained to me that some was hers but most of it was her husband's. Her husband had recently had a heart attack and was on quite a bit of medicine. Having had a terrible car accident a few years earlier, I was put on anti-depressants as well as sleeping pills, so I knew, first hand, how disorienting these medicines could be. I explained to him that although I did not feel that she was going to purposely try to kill herself, I did not feel it was safe in the state she was in to be leaving all those bottles out. I felt that they needed to be put away and her medication needed to be given to her when needed.

Later that night, I received a phone call from the boy's sister. She had spoken to her mother and she wanted to know if she could come see me. Of course I said yes. When she arrived she was very grateful that I allowed her to come and she went on to explain to me that earlier in the day when I had stopped at the house she had just left; I had just missed her. She was taking her father to the airport. Apparently the husband was the mother's second husband. The boy's natural father had been at the house but had to leave that morning to catch a flight home. *Oh my God*, I thought to myself. That is why he was so insistent that I go that morning! He wanted me to talk to both parents'.

I went on to tell the sister every detail I could remember about what he had told me throughout the week. His sister was able to validate a lot of the information I had received. He had been dating someone for a while and had discussed marriage but always seemed to postpone it; this time she said he was serious. She also told me that they were looking into a problem with the bike. It seems the bike had two gas tanks and they believe he was leaning over and trying to switch tanks when he crashed. That would definitely explain what I saw with the throttle and the looking down and then looking up and seeing myself going off the road. She was thrilled with all of the information I gave her, and quite honestly, at that point I was just happy to not be in jail.

Weeks later I received a phone call asking me about the dresser. They had found a shirt of his that his girlfriend used to wear but it wasn't in the top right drawer, it was on the right hand side of the room. The family wondered if that could be what he was referring too. I didn't know but it sounded close enough to me.

I believe it was a few months later that a neighbor would call to tell me that the mom had called her and asked her to give me a message. They were cleaning out his apartment when in the dresser in the right hand back of the top draw they found a life insurance policy payable to the girlfriend! Apparently that is what he wanted her to have!

To this day, this was without a doubt one of the most incredible experiences I have ever had with someone who has passed. The strength and determination of this boy to contact his family was too strong to be ignored. I still think about him and his family. There have been many times where I am overwhelmed and questioning my sanity, but whenever that happens, I always think back to the boy and the motorcycle and how his message brought peace to his entire family!

You are never forgotten.

One Gold Rose

I had first met my client, Judy, years ago when she came to me for a reading. Her husband, the love of her life, had passed. Like many of the clients I read for, she was looking for some validation that her husband was okay. Judy became a regular client of mine and I began seeing her on a monthly basis for Reiki healing sessions (Reiki is a form of hands-on-healing).

Years later, I was doing a Reiki healing session on her; it was right before Valentines Day. As I began the session I immediately felt the presence of her husband. This was not unusual, as he loved to stop in every now and again just to let her know he was still around her. He told me, as he always did, to tell her that he loved her. Then he told me something that I found rather confusing. He told me to tell her that he was sending her flowers and he showed me a gold rose. Now, because Judy had known me for years I had no problem telling her what he had told me. Of course, neither one of us could figure out how he would be sending flowers from the other side. We both just laughed and didn't discuss it any further.

A short time later I received a call from Judy. She was very excited as she went on to tell me the story. Apparently her priest who she hadn't heard from in years had mailed her a just thinking of you card.

She was shocked when she opened the card and found that on the front was a picture of a beautiful bouquet of flowers. What a wonderful gift! But that wasn't the best part. When she opened the card there it was: A gold lapel pin; and you guessed it, it was in the shape of a rose!

I cannot tell you how many of these stories I have heard; how many clients have called after their reading sessions to tell me about the amazing validations they have received. Our loved ones are around us all the time and they love to make their presence known. All they ask is that we pay attention.

The gift of humor can be taken with you to the "other side."

Duckie, Duckie, Duckie

It is very important to me that when I sit down with a client I have no idea who they are or why they are coming to me. As a psychic and medium, my job is to simply pass along the information I receive as accurately as possible. It is not my job to understand the message. And I have to tell you that many, many times I have no idea what the message means. This was definitely one of those times.

Nancy was a young girl who lost her father way too soon in life. He was very easy to communicate with and was quite chatty. As I tried to keep up with all the information, I began seeing a very funny image in my head. I kept seeing a white duck waddling back and forth across a street. As this vision continued, I also began hearing the words Duckie, Duckie, Duckie. I couldn't help but laugh as I passed along this silly vision that I was seeing in my head. Nancy told me she had no idea of what it meant but she would definitely keep it in mind.

As she left, we both had one last chuckle about the duck and as she walked out the door I told her to call me if she ever figured it out. It wasn't too long after that she called. She had gone home and was telling her mother all about the reading and the contact she had made with her father. She even told her mother about the Duckie, Duckie, Duckie. She couldn't believe it when her mother told her that her father was in the service and his nickname was none other than DUCKIE!

Many times when clients come for a reading, information will come through that neither I, nor they, can make sense of. As in the case of the Duckie story, it took another family member to validate the image. I love when this happens. So many times skeptics will say to me, "Well how do you know you aren't just reading the minds of the client?" Great question! However, it is impossible to read something in someone's mind that they never knew?

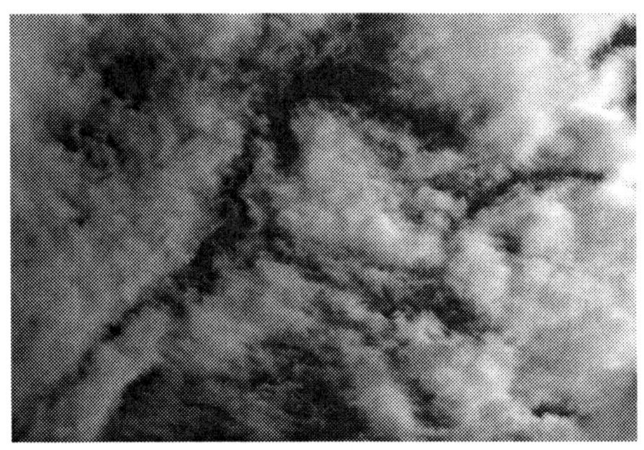

Survival is a skill you don't know you have till you need it.

Grandma Jennie Saves the Day

People ask me all the time, "What do you say to people that don't believe in any of this life after death stuff?" My response is always the same, "I'll see you on the other side and you will owe me a big apology."

I have had the amazing blessing of meeting many, many people who have had first hand experiences with deceased loved ones, angels, and spirit guides. I have also had many of these experiences myself. This particular experience I am going to share changed my life forever.

My son, 9, my daughter, 4, and I were heading home. It was Fri Oct 9, 1999. I was on a major highway with a speed limit of 65 mph. It was wet, raining on and off, there was a lot of traffic due to the holiday weekend, and I was driving my little Mercury Mystique. We were just a mile or so from our exit when suddenly, in my rearview mirror, I saw a car right on my back bumper. He was so close that I jumped when I caught the glimpse of him (for the sake of the story I will refer to the other driver as "he" and "him"). I immediately put on my blinker and prepared to move over into the right lane. Unfortunately, there was a Ryder Moving Truck that was right along side of me and I was unable to switch lanes. By now the man behind me was frantically flashing his lights and waving at me.

I waved back and pointed to the truck trying to make him understand I couldn't go anywhere. He was now so close that I was unable to see his license plate. I was terrified he was going to hit us. I made the decision to speed up and pass the Ryder truck so I could move over and get out of his way. As I passed the truck I soon realized there was another car in front of it. He was still right on my tail. I had to get out of the way, so I squeezed myself between the truck and the other vehicle. I waited for him to pass. It seemed like it took forever and I remembering saying to my son, "Where is he, he was in such a hurry." My son informed me he was right along side of us, giving us dirty looks. I turned my head to the left and sure enough there he was. He rode along side of us just glaring, and then proceeded ahead.

I waited until he was far enough ahead and I returned to my lane. He was now about 2 car lengths ahead of us. Suddenly, he began to accelerate and take off. It was at this time I began to accelerate to resume my original speed. As my car started to pick up speed I saw his brake lights come on. I remember so vividly the anger I immediately felt. What a jerk, brake checking on a wet road. I will never forget the incredible pain I felt in the pit of my stomach when within a split second I realized he wasn't brake checking me, he was stopping.

I immediately pulled the wheel as hard as I could to the right and slammed my brakes. I couldn't believe it. Somehow I made it around him. My heart was pounding and the adrenalin was flowing.

I did it; I made it. I had somehow made it around him and was now riding side by side with him. Suddenly his car veered into my lane. His passenger side came smashing into my middle, back driver side. The impact sent us into a violent spin.

We were now spinning out of control at 65 miles an hour on a busy highway and the kids were screaming. All I could think about were all the tractor-trailers I had passed earlier. I knew we would be hit again and I was waiting for the sound of yet another impact. I wish I could tell you it was just like those things you see on TV when you watch as your life passes before your eyes, but it wasn't. I didn't have time to pray and I didn't have a life review. I remembered trying to remember what the date was. I couldn't believe I was going to die at 31 years of age with my two children in the car and over something so stupid. Time just seemed to stop. Although this all happened within seconds, to this day when I recount the events, I am amazed at ALL that took place within those few seconds. It was at that moment I heard the voice.

The voice spoke gently but firmly and was quite loud. "Listen to me," said the voice, "No matter what you do, do not let go of the wheel." "Hold on as tight as you can. If you hit your head you won't be able to get the kids out, just hold on." I immediately began screaming to the children. Hold on! Hold on as tight as you can! The children were screaming out of control. We were still spinning and there was nothing I could do.

I had closed my eyes and was waiting to feel the next impact from one of the vehicles behind me. I opened my eyes and saw the car heading for a guardrail. On the other side was a 20-foot drop and we were heading straight for it.

I still cannot fully explain what happened next. I remember knowing I was going to die. I remember my only thought was of my children. Why did they have to be in the car with me? The next thing I remember was an incredible feeling of falling. I was sure we had broken through the guardrail and I could feel us falling. Then there was a loud bang.

I do not know if I lost consciousness. I remember such quiet. I remember thinking, am I dead? I think I am dead. I was so confused. Then I heard my son screaming uncontrollably, "Mommie, don't die, Mommie don't leave us, you can't leave us." He just kept saying it over and over and over in an angry tone, as if I went somewhere without him. I then felt a coldness dripping down my face. I remember thinking, well I must be alive if I feel that, but why is he screaming like that? I slowly opened my eyes.

The air bag was still deflating and as it came down I could see out the front windshield. I couldn't believe my eyes. The roof of my car and windshield had caved in and was now about six inches from my forehead. Lined up right where the roof and windshield met was the guardrail.

The car was filled with smoke and I was beginning to panic. I heard the voice again, "You are okay, stay calm, you are okay, the smoke is from the air bag, stay calm and don't panic."

I now heard my son again, still screaming and struggling to get out of his seat belt. He was screaming that he had to get out and was trying to climb out the window that had blown out during the impact. It was at this moment that I realized I hadn't heard anything from my daughter. I immediately became nauseous and panic filled my entire being. Fear took over. I remember thinking okay what do I want here. I can't pick one child to live. I can't lose one of my children. If one of us goes then I hope we all go. I heard the voice again, "You need to calm down, take a deep breath and turn around." "I don't want to," I said. I was sure we had gone over the cliff. I was sure my daughter had been thrown from the car. I did not want to turn around. "Turn around," the voice said, this time more firmly. I closed my eyes, took a deep breath and turned around.

If I live to be 100 years old and suffer from Alzheimer's I will never forget what I saw next. I turned around and saw my two beautiful children, my precious gifts from God, sitting in white lights. They were untouched. It was as if someone lifted them out of the car, let the car crash, and then slipped them back in. The impact was so severe that all the windows on the left side were blown out. There was glass everywhere. Any loose items in the car had been thrown all over, yet the children didn't have a scratch on them. I kept telling them, "We are okay, our angels are here and they were taking care of us."

By now my son was half out the window. I realized I if I could crawl out of my seat I could get out the passenger side. I swung the door opened and climbed out. I was absolutely shocked to find out we hadn't gone off the cliff. The car had come to rest right on the side of the highway. I watched in shock as all these cars and trucks went buzzing by. There I was covered in blood, standing on the side of a major highway screaming for help. It seemed like no one would stop. I couldn't believe no one was stopping. I felt a hand on my shoulders and turned around to see the man in the Ryder truck. As he helped me around my car, I turned to look at the damage of the car. My knees went weak and I felt myself falling to the ground; my body began trembling and I was overwhelmed by emotion.

My car was lodged under the guardrail. The car had hit the guardrail and spun around taking out 7 guardrail posts. The impact blew out all the windows on the left side, and the wheels on the left side had actually caved under the frame of the car. The driver's door was smashed in but the window frame had torn out, leaving hanging metal. My car was facing against the traffic. A garage door remote control that had been on the visor was thrown 15 feet from the car and all that was left were little electronic pieces.

Earlier that day my daughter had gotten a school box filled with scissors and crayons. The box, crayons, and scissors were thrown from the vehicle and were now scattered all over the highway. The most shocking sight was the front tire that stopped literally inches from the edge of the cliff. The hood had lifted up and was actually caught in the guardrail. All the rescue people kept telling me how "lucky" I was to be alive. They (unnecessarily) informed me that if the car had gone another few inches, the guardrail, which was lined up perfectly with my forehead, would have killed me instantly.

We had just got home from the emergency room and the children, my mother, and I were sitting around the table, the kids were eating. Now I need to explain that in our house we are very open about what mommy does for a living. My daughter is very gifted herself and since the age of two (before I became involved on my Spiritual path) she would tell detailed stories about angels and heaven. My grandmother, Jennie, had passed away 4 1/2 years before my daughter was born. Yet, my daughter would tell you very detailed information about her great-grandmother and she insists to this day that she lived with her in heaven. So when I asked them the following question I expected a YES. I asked the children if they saw angels when we crashed. To my shock they both said no!

It was then my daughter, with a mouth full of food, said, "But I did see Grandma Jennie." My mother pursued it further. "What do you mean you saw Grandma Jennie?" my mom asked. "I saw Grandma Jennie when we crashed," she said quite indignantly. She went on to explain, "I saw Grandma Jennie when we crashed. She was by the engine." "The engine," my mother said. "Yes," my daughter said, quite annoyed. "She was by mommy's head, pushing the engine," she explained.

The only reason I am alive today is because when the car went under the guardrail the hood popped open and caught the guardrail, stopping it where it did. If that hood didn't come up I would be dead. Some call it luck. I say THANK YOU Grandma Jennie, our angels, and guides. It obviously wasn't our time to go, and divine intervention made sure we would stay right here!

Driver Follow-Up

Whenever I share this story I am always asked what happened to the driver that caused the accident so I am going to take a moment to digress from our Spiritual topic and give you the follow up.

He never stopped. He left the scene of the accident. I thank God everyday that we did not go over that embankment and that the car did not catch fire because no one would have noticed us. The driver returned ONE HOUR later as we were pulling away in the ambulance. He was ticketed for causing the accident but not for leaving the scene. Apparently he convinced the police that he went to get help. The interesting thing is the accident occurred directly across from a police station on the opposite side of the highway. The next exit was also only a mile away. I have never bought his pathetic story! I believe he was drunk and went to sober up before returning to the scene which would be validated for me later on.

I was literally a mess after the accident. I had severe problems with my stomach that would last almost 2 years. I was told the problem was a direct result of the severe stress I suffered from the accident. I constantly played the accident over and over and over in my head. I was always recreating the accident and wondering if I had just done this or done that if it wouldn't have happened. I couldn't live with knowing that I may have done something wrong which almost resulted in losing my children.

I was in my lawyer's office one day and I was in my usually hysterics and crying uncontrollable which seemed to be the norm those days. The lawyer pulled out a stack of printed out papers about an inch thick. He handed them to me and told me to look at them closely. To my amazement they were the DMV records on the man that caused the accident. It was VERY clear in reading through the endless list of offenses that the man had a drinking problem. He literally had tickets in every town in the county. Of course most of them had been pleaded down to minor offenses. He had license restrictions, suspensions, and I was shocked to find out after all of those offenses he had just gotten his license back about a month before he caused my accident.

Then something happened that would change everything for me. The lawyer opened a bottom draw in his desk and took out a stack of pictures. He looked at me and said "I am not going to show these to you because no one should ever have to see the things in these pictures. But I will tell you this: these are pictures of cars that were in accidents and they have less than half of the damage that your car had. The people in these cars did not survive. I am showing you the DMV records to show you once and for all that you were in no way responsible for this accident and you need to stop tormenting yourself. The fact that you walked away from this accident is amazing. You are obviously here for a reason so you need to do whatever you can to get yourself better."

I never did get a dime from that accident. As a matter of fact my insurance company paid the other driver $500! My car was totaled and I wasn't even reimbursed the full amount I owed. Insurance companies; that is an entirely different book!

He did eventually have to go to court for the ticket and I was notified. I will tell you that I have never understood until that day why people who have loved ones who are murdered or victimized feel the need to sit in the court room and face the criminal. But there is a certain power you take back in facing someone who has taken something from you, who has wronged you or has caused you tremendous pain.

On that day I walked into the courtroom with a mission. I was one of the first to arrive and picked a seat out of the about 100 seats that were in the court room. As the universe would have it, he would wind up sitting directly behind me. It became very apparent that he had no idea who I was, but I would never forget his face. I sat in the courtroom with my stomach flipping as he sat there next to his mother. My blood boiled as he went on and on about how pissed off he was that he had to be inconvenienced and come to court. He also was telling his mother how he heard that now "the bitch" was trying to sue him. I couldn't believe my ears! Did this man not have any remorse for what he had done? Even if you unintentionally caused an accident like that wouldn't you be overcome with regretful ness and compassion for the suffering you caused? I just sat there gripping the picture I was holding in my hand of my two children. I was there for me. I was there for them. I was there to face the man who single handily almost took all of our lives!

He was eventually called up to the front of the court to give his plea. I decided to take that opportunity to turn around and face his mother. I asked her if she was the mother of and I said his name. She quickly and proudly said yes. I reached out my hand to shake hers. I told her I was the girl that her son almost killed. I held up the picture of my two children and told her these were my two beautiful children who were also in the car that day. She immediately began telling me how sorry he was. How not a day goes by that he is not feeling bad. She went on to tell me how he hadn't slept through the night since the accident and how all he could think about were my two sons. Okay I have a son and a daughter! Was this woman kidding me? Did she not realize I was sitting there the entire time listening to this cold hearted, irresponsible excuse for a human being?

As his mother continued pleading his case to me I saw him coming back to his seat. I had a big smile on my face as I did not want to tip him off as to whom I was. I could see the confusion in his eyes as he tried to place where he knew me from. He looked at me and I continued smiling. "You have no idea who I am, do you?" I asked. "No," he replied with a little giggle. "Well please allow me to introduce myself." My stomach was churning and I could feel every cell in my body shaking as I reached my hand to his. I don't know where I found the courage, but I firmly gripped his hand in mine and said, "I am Lisa, Lisa Ann, you know the girl you almost killed along with her children. I just want you to know that I know all about you and I will be watching you because you will NEVER do this to anyone ever again." I didn't say anything about what I knew about his driving record or his alcohol problem as my lawyer has sworn me to secrecy because the information was confidential. At that point, his mother freaked out and began yelling how he is not an alcoholic anymore and he goes to AA. She made such as scene that they were both immediately escorted out of the courtroom.

Do you know to this day I don't know what happened with the ticket? In all of the commotion I never heard what the judge said. Honestly though, it didn't matter. I had done what I came there to do. I had looked him in the eye! I had taken back my power!

This is what was left of the car!

54

Free Will

To Stay or to Go

Mary had been a client of mine for several years. Her father had died and she would come about once a year to check in with him. I loved communicating with her father because he was so easy to talk to. It was just like talking to a living person and he had a great sense of humor. When she called, I was sure it was to schedule her yearly appointment to chat with her dad, but when she began to speak I could hear the stress in her voice and I could feel her fear. She told me she needed my help. She went onto tell me that her brother had been in a horrible car accident and was in a coma. She was terrified and she didn't know if he was going to make it. She wasn't sure if I could help her, but she was desperate for any information I could give her. I myself had no idea what I could do, but I knew she needed my help.

I asked for her brother's name, closed my eyes, and tried to connect with him. For the sake of the story I will refer to him as Joe. As soon as I closed my eyes I immediately saw two figures. I was instantly aware that I was connecting with her father who I had spoken to many, many times. I was shocked when I realized that the other figure was indeed her brother. I instantly felt panicked as I tried to figure out how I was going to tell her that her brother had died. I was thinking that there is no way I could possibly deliver this kind of news over the phone. Then suddenly Joe began to speak.

He told me that he was scared and he didn't know what to do. He told me that he was there with his dad. He went on to tell me that the accident was his entire fault and that if he came back everyone would hate him. I assured him that he was loved very much and no one would hate him. I knew it was his free will choice and all I could do at this point was to reassure him and remind him of how much he was loved.

I passed on all of the information I got to his sister. I explained to her that it was very important that everyone around him tell him that they love him and that they were not mad at him. I explained to her that I could not make any promises as he had free will choice and the only thing I could do was pass on the information. I couldn't stress enough to her how important it was to keep telling him he was loved and forgiven. The rest would be his choice.

His sister informed me that his car accident was the result of drugs and alcohol that had ended in a police chase through several towns. The chase came to end when he finally crashed into a gas station and almost blew up a small town. I was horrified, but yet I now understood where his guilt and fear of being judged was coming from.

I am not sure how long after that, as my memory with dates is not what it used to be, but the sister contacted me again. She said that she needed me to try to connect with her brother and get whatever information I could. Once again I closed my eyes and focused on his name. I immediately connected with him, however, this time he was not on the other side, but standing by himself. He never spoke, but I saw visions of him learning to walk and talk. I was thrilled with this vision because I figured it meant he had decided to stay. I eagerly shared this great news with his sister. She was rather confused. She informed me that although her brother was still in a coma there was no brain damage and no physical damage. In fact, the doctors could find nothing wrong with him except that he was still in a coma. I told her I couldn't really explain it but I was encouraged because I felt it meant that he would be waking up soon. She seemed very concerned about the fact that I saw him learning how to talk and walk, as there was currently no reason that would be happening.

Sometime later I was called to do a reading party. Now normally I do not go to anyone's house unless I know how he or she was referred to me, but for some reason, in all the times I spoke to this woman, I never asked her how she got my name. When I arrived at the house she told me that she wanted me to do her reading first before all the other guests arrived. During her reading it came up that she had a son in the hospital. I don't really recall all the details, but we spent most of the reading talking about her son. After the reading she looked at me and said, "I was told you do not like to know anything about your clients before you read for them and you especially don't want to know if they are connected to someone you have already read for." She went on. She told me that she was the mother of Joe the boy in the coma.

She told me that what I didn't know was that the last time the sister called me, the doctors were trying to convince her to just give up on the son, saying that he was never going to wake up. They wanted her to disconnect him from the life support. She told me that she felt he would wake up and the information I gave the sister in that second call validated that for her. And to my excitement she told me that he did indeed wake up a short time after. While he has no brain damage he unfortunately got a horrible staph infection in the hospital and was left with no speech and was paralyzed on one side. "It was exactly what you said. You saw him learning to walk and talk. We didn't understand what you meant at the time but now we do." She went on to tell me that he was having a very difficult time and rehab was becoming nearly impossible. She said the only words they understood where usually curse words and the hospital staff was at a loss of what to do next. His violent behavior and bad attitude had brought his rehabilitation to a stand still.

I don't remember if she asked me or if I offered, but we decided that I would take a trip to see him. He was at a rehabilitation center about 2 hours from where I lived. It was a long drive so I decided to take another healer with me. This time I would not be visiting as a psychic but as a healer. On the drive up I told the entire story to my friend who was also a healer. I will call him Alex.

Alex was new to the world of healing and Reiki and while he was very supportive of my work, I could see the doubt in his face. He very politely asked me what I was thinking and how I thought I would be able to help when the even trained medical staff couldn't get near him. I had a theory that I couldn't wait to test. I, of course, had no idea if it would work, but in my line of work you always need to be up to the challenges that you come across. I explained to Alex that it was my belief that I had spoken directly to

Joe on those two occasions when I was asked to connect with him by his sister. I had this crazy thought that since he had already met me on the soul/spirit level he would somehow recognize me and allow me to work on him. I believed that by doing some healing on him I would be able to release some of the hurt, fear, and frustration, therefore allowing the medical staff the ability to work with him. Alex very politely looked at me and said, "I hope you have a plan B." We both laughed.

Joe's mother met us at the hospital entrance and was visibly shaken. She informed us that Joe was having a very bad day and no one had been able to get near him. She apologized and said how horrible she felt that I had driven all that way for nothing. I spoke with her briefly and pointed out that since I was there I should at least try to see what I could do.

She finally agreed and up to the room we went. Now I have to tell you, as always, I had no idea what I was doing or if my great idea would even work. People depend on me for strength, guidance, support, and help and I was not about to let this family down. So I put my own fear aside, took a deep breath, and entered the room while everyone else cautiously stood outside the door. I walked slowly up to the bed and in a relaxed voice I said, "Hi Joe, I am Lisa Ann, a friend of your sister, Mary. It is such a pleasure to finally meet you." As I prepared for the yelling, hitting, or whatever else, the most amazing thing happened. Joe looked at me and with a tear in his eye, reached out, and took my hand. He pulled my hand to his mouth, gently kissed it, and placed it over his heart. I couldn't believe what was happening! While I pretended to have all the confidence in the world, I honestly had no clue as to whether or not my insane plan would work. But it did! And there I was standing right next to the hospital bed with Joe holding my hand.

My friend Alex and I worked on Joe for about an hour. We even showed his daughter, who I believe was around 5 or 6, how to send her father some healing energy. Last I heard, Joe was well on his way to recovery. He had a very long road ahead of him but he was alive and that is all that mattered! He had made the decision to stay and not to go!

Determination

Sept 11th - A Son's Message to His Dad

I don't think there is anyone out there who doesn't remember where they were on 9-11-2001, the day of the most terrible terrorist attacks on the US. It was a day that has changed our lives forever. I live only one hour from New York City and on the day of the attack I had a boyfriend who was going to school in Manhattan and a sister who was overseas in Europe for work. I am thankful that I personally did not lose anyone in the tragedy, however, I indirectly knew of many people who lost loved ones. My heart goes out to all who lost someone on that terrible day.

It was a week or so before Christmas when I received a frantic phone call from a client of mine. She informed me that a co-worker of hers had lost a son in the 9-11 tragedy and he, the co-worker, was in a horrible space. She wanted to know if there was anyway I could read for him as soon as possible, as his family and friends were very concerned about him. Of course I agreed and an appointment was set up.

When the father called I gave him my usual "Don't give me any information" speech and I explained how the process worked. I was able to instantly connect with his son, Chris, and he was very eager to talk to his father. Chris went on and on about many different things.

Although the father was very skeptical, he was thrilled with the reading and did not understand how I could possibly know all of the things I was saying. I assured him I knew nothing and was simply repeating what Chris was telling me. The father was able to validate everything I was telling him and as the reading continued, I could feel a sense of peace overcoming him.

It was towards the end of the reading that Chris informed me that he had been trying very hard to communicate with his dad, but his dad was very stubborn and so devastated that it was hard for him to get through. He told me to tell his dad that he would continue trying and that he should pay attention to the messages he was sending. Chris was one determined spirit! He then told me that there was a baby coming down and he was very excited about it. The father immediately stopped me. He said that while everything else I told him made perfect sense, this information did not. He assured me that there was absolutely no one around him that could possibly be announcing a pregnancy. I explained to him that it didn't necessarily need to be a family member and that he should just put the information in the back of his mind and that it would eventually make sense.

A few weeks later, the father called me again to ask me if I thought the thing about the pregnancy could have been something to do with a miscarriage. While I do sometimes pick up on miscarriages, I assured the father that in this instance that was not the case. In a miscarriage I will see the baby going up and this baby was very clearly coming down, which meant a birth. He thanked me for my time and told me that the reading had helped him to get through the holiday.

A few weeks after that, I received another call from Chris's father, he sounded very excited father. He told me that a woman his son worked with had called him to tell him about a dream she had about his son. He was very excited as he went on to tell me that everything in her dream matched exactly what I had told him weeks before. He couldn't believe it. Then he took a deep breath and continued. "You are not going to believe this," he said. Right before the woman hung up she told him again how terribly sorry she was for his loss. She said that she wanted to share some good news with him. "I just found out that I am pregnant!" The father was overwhelmed with joy. The one piece of information that he just could not understand from the first reading now all made sense! He was thrilled! I cried, he cried. I was so happy for him and was assured that now he would be able to get even more messages from his son.

It is important to understand the way energy works. When we are alive we vibrate at a certain level. When we die we vibrate at a much higher level. Those of us, like me, who communicate with the dead, are able to lift our vibration thus making it easier for those on the other side to communicate with us. This is done through meditation and quieting the mind. It is something that anyone can learn to do. Unfortunately, when people are grieving the loss of a loved one it lowers their vibration, making it very difficult for the person who has passed to communicate. In many cases the grieving person mistakenly thinks that this lack of communication is because the person who has passed is upset with them. They continue to become more and more depressed, which lowers their vibration even more making it nearly impossible for the person who has passed to communicate with them. A vicious cycle begins. I try to explain this to people who are in deep grief so that they can understand what they need to do in order to be able to connect and be open to the communications from their loved ones.

The loss of a loved one is a horrible thing. I always tell people that on their worst grieving day when they wonder how they will go on, they need to remember this: there is nothing more our loved ones want than for us to be happy. When we die we understand why everything has happened. Time on the other side is very different than our time and our loved ones on the other side know they will be reunited with us very soon.

If you are grieving the loss of a loved one, I want you to think about what you would want if the situation were reversed. If you were on the other side and your loved one was still here, you would want them to go on and have the happiest life they could because you know you will see them again. That is what they want for us. They want us to be happy and to continue moving forward. They want us to know that when it is our time, they will be there to greet us.

As there are no such things as coincidences, just as I was putting the finishing touches on my book, Chris' father called me for another reading. It had been several years since my last reading with him. Once again, Chris came through with lots to say. He even helped us with a special recipe he had for cooking vegetables that his dad was longing for. As with many readings some of the stuff that came through wasn't clicking immediately with his dad.

Before I hung up, I told Chris' dad about my book and asked him if he would like me to send him a copy of the story about his son. I was honored to have him read it and was thrilled to have him add anything else he could remember about that first reading session. Here is the actual email I received a day or two following the reading with Chris' dad. The last names have been omitted to protect the privacy of these families and the email has been included with the consent of Chris' dad.

Dear Lisa Ann,

Thank you for sending the chapter to me. Feel free to refer to Chris as Chris or Christopher.

When I spoke to you the other night you mentioned that Chris was with Bobby. It took a while to penetrate but I eventually realized that was Bobby "L" who was in the same fire company as Chris. I am always told that Chris is with him. You also mentioned an older man named Peter who I thought might be Chris' lieutenant. I checked that when I got off the phone and it is correct. You also mentioned a Steve. I thought it might have been his friend or brother in law but you said it was someone who crossed over. As soon as I woke the next day I remembered that the remaining firefighter from Chris' company was Steve "R". You batted three for three. It's a comfort to know he is with his "brothers" even now. Chris wouldn't want to be anywhere else.

In our first conversation *(the first reading I ever did for him)* you mentioned that Chris was helped to cross over by a man in uniform who had been there *(meaning on the other side)* before 9/11. That was a very good friend of my family who was a firefighter with me. He had passed with cancer several years before 9/11.

Also that first time you said that Chris was mentioning the end of April or the beginning of May. His birthday is May 8th.

You might want to mention in that chapter that quite a few people had come to you after 9/11 attempting to hear from someone they lost on that day and that Chris was such a strong spirit that he was the first one that was able to come through.

A lot of the other things that my daughter's friend dreamt validated things that you said, such as that Chris went very quick, he was helping other people, etc.

Thank you for the comfort you gave me,

Mike

Once again, I am amazed at the power and strength of the love that penetrates through from the other side! I need to add that in all the readings I have done for the families of 9/11, there is one common message that has always come through. That message is that NO SOUL, NO SOUL crossed over alone. It is my very strong belief that as the souls passed one by one, they all waited around the site until the last soul was ready to cross.

To all of you who have lost love ones in that tragic event know this: Your loved ones have touched the souls of so many here. There is not a day that goes by that someone here is not thinking of them. We make better choices in our lives, we make sure we enjoy every moment to the fullest, we appreciate our friends and families, and we strive to be the best we can. We do all of this because we have been so touched by their stories and your loss. Our hearts go out to you. Our prayers are always with you. Know that your loved ones have truly made a difference in our lives!

Do you believe everything you read in the history books?

The Meucci Haunting
Re-writing History

A few years ago I was at my parents' house for the holiday. My aunt (my father's sister), uncle, and Cousin Brian were also there. During dinner, my aunt proudly announced that my cousin had his own TV show and that she had brought a DVD of the show. Of course we were all very excited. My mother asked her what the show was about. "Well you are probably going to think this is nuts," my aunt said, "But Brian and his friends investigate haunted sights," she responded. I remember almost spitting my drink across the table. "Do you know what I do for a living?" I asked. "No," they all responded. "I am a psychic, for the love of God!" I replied. We all had a good laugh.

We couldn't believe the coincidence that both of us were doing such similar work! Obviously we hadn't seen each other for a few years, so we spent the rest of the time swapping stories. We continued to keep in touch for the next couple of years and we always said someday we would work together. I was so excited the day I got the email from Brian asking me if I would be willing to come to Staten Island to do an investigation with him and his team. Of course I said yes!

As with every reading or investigation I do, I made it very clear that I did not want to know anything about the investigation. I didn't even want to know where we were going (It is very important that I do not have any prior knowledge of events, places, or people before I arrive, as it will influence what I get. The less I know the more accurate I can be). I was given a date, a time, and directions to my cousin's apartment on Staten Island. My cousin is the "the forever-skeptic scientist," so he was thrilled to accommodate my "no information" request. He has worked with psychics in the past but always questioned the validity of the information they gave him, as they knew way ahead of time where they were going. Since many of the sights had a lot of history to them, it was very easy for one to simply research the locations online ahead of time. He was thrilled that I was not from Staten

Island and I would have no knowledge of where I was going. He felt this would allow for a more controlled investigation.

I arrived in Staten Island that afternoon and I am happy to report that I made it without making one U-turn. Sorry, I had to add that. As psychic as I am, I am horrible with directions, so I consider it a major accomplishment when I arrive somewhere without making one hundred U-turns. I met my cousin at his apartment, we went and had a nice lunch, and then it was back to the apartment to grab a ton of equipment.

We arrived at the site around 3pm. It was the Garibaldi Museum; I was so excited! I had just seen the movie Night at the Museum with Ben Stiller. For those of you who haven't seen the movie, it is about a museum where everyone comes to life at night (a great movie with a lot of information about history). I could not wait to get the investigation underway!

As we walked through the gates I immediately started seeing images of people scattered on the front lawn. I felt like they were there getting treatment for injuries, and that at one point the lawn was used as a makeshift triage. I also kept getting a vision in my mind's eye of tomb stones and was sure that there was a cemetery right there, but I kept looking and didn't see anything. I also felt like there were a couple of bodies buried on the property, possibly two or three, and something about unmarked graves. I kept getting a feeling of the cemetery in the back left hand corner of the property.

As we entered the museum I was instantly taken over by a very anxious feeling. I saw a room to my right, a long hallway with the staircase facing away from us, and a sign-in podium right in front of us. I remember thinking to myself that I want to go downstairs, but there was no downstairs! I was immediately taken into a room where some of the other team members were already waiting with another local ghost investigating team. Everyone was told to not speak about anything having to do with the museum, because the "psychic" had arrived. I was introduced to everyone and was told that Greg would be walking through with me on my investigation.

He would be the skeptic asking me questions and interviewing me as we went along. I have to tell you, for someone as impatient as me, the next couple of hours were a killer; I sat there waiting for all of the equipment to be set up and other interviews to be taped, which took place upstairs where there was no way anyone else could hear what was being said. I could not wait to get started!

I have to tell you that I was very impressed by the way that the entire investigation was handled. Brian goes out of his way to keep the investigation as controlled as possible. Three teams were assigned. Greg and I would be the first team to go through and investigate. Greg would interview me and ask me questions as we went through. My cousin and another ghost investigator would be the next team to investigate. They would be the team that did the scientific part of the investigation. They had all the toys a ghost investigator could ever want: three different EMF meters (electro-magnetic field), digital audio recorder (to pick up EVPs -electronic voice phenomena), as well as a digital non-contact thermometer. Finally, the last team, which consisted of a "Sensitive" (meaning he didn't claim to be psychic, however he did pick up on the feelings of places) and a cameraman, would go through. There were several different cameras that were placed throughout the house and all the tapes were changed after each investigation. All in all, I was blown away.

The room I was in had two doorways, one at the front of the house and one towards the back. I was in that room for hours just trying to keep everything blocked off until it was time for me to begin. I tried not to allow myself to psychically pick up on anything before the taping, so I sat there trying to ignore the visions I was getting. It is very important that I stick with my first impressions and do not try to analyze the information too much, but, hard as I tried, I couldn't help but notice this man who kept peeking in on me from the back hallway.

Finally, I couldn't take it anymore; no matter how hard I tried to block it out I kept getting feelings and impressions of things. I decided to grab a piece of paper and start writing some stuff down. Of course I didn't bring any paper with me, so I stepped out of the room to grab one of the blank sign-in sheets. As I was pulling a piece of paper out of the binder I looked down and noticed doors in the floor that lead to the basement! The podium that held the sign-in sheet had hid them. I was so excited and could not wait to get down there. Of course Greg had noticed my departure from the room and came out to see where I had gone. I told him I HAD to get into that basement; he assured me I would be allowed down there but for now I had to return to the room. I grabbed my paper and went back to the set up room.

These following entries are the original notes I had jotted down before the investigation:

-upon entering lawn, lots of people, anxious feeling, make-shift triage on lawn.

-inside drawn to back door, saw man in uniform keeps peeking at me.

-as darkness falls energy shifting in this place, entering, meeting place, secret group, society, met in the cover of night

-when I walked in hallway I kept feeling I need to go into the basement, but there is no staircase down, then when I went to grab the paper at sign-in desk I noticed the floorboards that open to the basement- I NEED to go down there.

-as I am writing there is a man behind me on my left hand side watching me, feel very lightheaded and spacey

-children hid out here

FINALLY, it was show time! Greg and I joined Chris, the camera guy (another skeptic). I was nervous, but as always, up for a challenge. Before we got started my biggest concern was how horrible my hair looked after being in and out of the rain all day. By this time I had waited so long that my mind began to wander to thoughts of why I had to eat that entire bag of chips and why I didn't start my Pilates a few weeks sooner. But no more time to focus on that. Now it was time to go.

We went back outside and we started from the beginning. By this time it was dark and the energy of the place had really shifted. We went back out to the sidewalk and began filming as Greg and I walked up the sidewalk making our way to the museum. I started by relaying what I had felt upon arrival. I shared the vision I had earlier of the people on the lawn and the persistent feeling that there was a cemetery somewhere close.

As we entered the house I was again taken over by that same anxiousness. I cannot explain how strong the feeling I was getting about going into that basement. I had to get down there! As I slowly and carefully climbed down the steep steps I could begin to feel the anxiety leaving with each step I took. As I got closer to the basement, I felt this feeling of safety and relief coming over me. As I stepped off the last step I was immediately drawn to the back right hand corner of the basement. As I made my way to the back corner I was overcome by a feeling of "I made it, I am safe." I felt that people, families, even children had made it to that same spot many times. I felt that they were seeking shelter, and protection, but from what or who I did not know. I saw in my mind's eye some kind of underground tunnel or temporary underground hiding place. On the other side of the basement I saw homemade wine sitting in jars. Now it was time to make our way upstairs.

As I entered the hallway I was excited to once again see the man who had been peeking in on me still standing by the back door. He told me that his name was Marcus and he was the right hand man to who he called the "Big Man." He told me he was still here to look over and protect the place. He also confirmed for me the feeling of the secret meetings that I had gotten earlier. He told me that he greeted the people for these meetings and that they were indeed held at night and by invitation only. Greg joked about why, if he was there to greet people, he was standing at the back door. It didn't make any sense to me but I have learned to not question the other side.

There were two more rooms to the right of the front door. One was filled with some rather interesting art that was very distracting and did not seem to fit with the era of the home. The adjoining room was filled with pictures, relics, and an odd looking mask. There was also a piano and an incredible, unique chair. I didn't stop to look at anything, nor did I try to focus on anything specific. As I walked through, I got some quick visions of women in long dresses from what looked like the late 1800's. I have to tell, you it is times like this when I really wish I had paid better attention in history class! I also felt like there were a lot of parties held there for people who were higher up in the community.   Now it was time to head upstairs.

The first room I entered was currently set up as the curator's office. As I entered the room I was overcome with sadness. I saw the image of an elderly woman. I felt this woman was very ill and had been bedridden for quite some time. I felt she had died of pneumonia and before her death she suffered from dementia. I saw her pacing the floor in circles and got the impression that she was looking for someone named Martha (possibly her nurse or caretaker). Greg asked me who she was and if I got a name. Although I did not feel that I was speaking to the women directly, I was audibly hearing information about her. I heard that she was the wife of the "Big Man" and all I saw was the letter "E," but I didn't get a name. I was also told, by whoever was speaking to me, that people in the museum hear footsteps and that those footsteps were hers. She still paces the floor in what once was her room. I made a mental note to myself so I would remember to ask the curator later on if people did indeed hear footsteps in that room.

The next room I entered was the staff office where all of the computers and other equipment were located. The energy of this room was totally different from the last room; it was very happy and bright. As I entered the room, I immediately felt the presence of a little boy and girl. The little boy showed me that they constantly move things around and love to have fun. He told me they died older but they loved this house and chose to come through at these ages and stay in the house and play. They weren't trying to scare anyone they were just having fun. He seemed very eager to take personal responsibility for all of the unexplained nonsense that happens in that room.

As we continued our investigation it was killing me to know if any of what I was getting was making any sense. But of course I would have to wait to find out. I entered another room currently used as a library. For some reason I didn't feel the need to stay in there and abruptly left. I wasn't getting a bad feeling; I just didn't feel like I needed to be there.

Next, I made my way to the final room on the upper floor. As I entered, I felt the presence of a very strong and big man. Could it be the "Big Man" I had heard so much about? I felt he was a very well-read man, intelligent beyond his time, a dreamer, a creator, a man with a vision. I felt he led or held a very high role in the secret society meetings I had felt earlier. I felt that he had a vision and these meetings were just the start. I felt that this was not just a religious thing, but that the people who came to these meetings (men only) were big players in the community. I felt that they pretty much controlled that area. Again, I got the feeling of these meetings being very secretive and only held at night. I felt that this man did not believe in the separation of church and state and that these meetings had just as strong of a religious base as a professional/business base. I had a very strong feeling that he was very active behind the scenes but he didn't always get the credit for his work. I also heard that he was a self-proclaimed visionary and a man way ahead of his time. He made me feel that this was his thinking room. He liked to read and think in this room. I also felt he was a dreamer and a lot of his visions came to him in his dreams. He then showed me that he was the person or ghost that people kept seeing in the house. He showed me that he comes as shadows and people would see him out of the corner of their eye. As I left the room I couldn't help but to feel very honored to have talked to this man. But I had no idea what I was about to find out.

I can't remember where I was in the house when I was getting a very strong impression of a boat or ship accident. It was very frustrating to me because it was obvious that the house was very old and I wasn't sure if everything that I was getting was connected or from different times. I tried very hard to just repeat whatever I was seeing, feeling, or hearing without trying to understand it. At some point, I had a feeling that there was a part of the house missing and kept seeing a brick wall with a wood stove. Before leaving the upper floor of the house, I had one last impression. I felt like someone needed to go up in the attic. I felt that there was something up there that needed to be found. But our part of the investigation was finished and it was time for the next team to begin. We were politely booted outside while the next team prepared to do their investigation.

While outside, I was introduced to the curator of the museum. She was very excited to hear what I had picked up on, as there had been several other psychics out there previously. I was thrilled and couldn't wait to tell her my findings. To my absolute astonishment she was able to confirm a lot of the information I had gotten, as well as fill in a lot of the blanks. I have tried to the best of my ability to recall that initial conversation with her and share all of the information she was able to validate. Rather than reiterate the conversation, I have decided to list what was validated room by room.

The Property
Mr. & Mr. Meucci owned the home. I was informed that the couple was actually buried on the property. There are two monuments, which I thought were part of the artwork of the museum (what do I know), but are actually the grave markers! They are located in the front of the museum on the right hand side. The curator told me that she has also felt that there is someone else buried on the property and she, too, felt it in the same back left hand corner. She also told me that they will be doing some work there over the summer and the lawn will need to be dug up. Who knows what they will find?

The Hallway
As we continued discussing my findings, Greg mentioned Marcus at the back door and asked if there was anyone by that name that

she knew of. She was not sure. As I saw Marcus watching over the house from the rear entrance, Greg continued laughing at the fact that he was standing at the wrong door. To our astonishment the curator informed us that Marcus wasn't standing at the back door, he was standing at the front door! Apparently the house had been moved twice, and the last time the house was moved, it was carried across the street. They didn't turn the house around, so the current back door was actually the original front door (ha – ha Greg)!

While we were on break waiting for the final team to get ready for their investigation, the curator took me into the museum part and showed me a picture of a group of men taken outside of the home. The picture was taken in the 1800's. One of the names listed under the photo was M. Lemmi. Could this be Marcus? A week or so after the original investigation, the curator was able to search through some records and found that M. Lemmi was actually Michael Lemmi not Marcus. It looks like the search for Marcus will continue.

The Basement
The curator informed us that another resident of the home was Giuseppe Garibaldi. Garibaldi was a nationalist and revolutionary. After the death of Garibaldi's wife, he was invited by Meucci to stay at the home. It was very possible that this was the link to the political refugees that I felt and to the underground tunnels or hide outs that offered sanctuary to those who needed it.

The Curators Office
She was able to confirm pretty much everything I felt in this room. There was indeed a woman in this house, who did stay in that room. Her name did begin with an "E." Esther or Esterre (in Italian) was the wife of Mr. Meucci. She was indeed bedridden for many years, suffering with arthritis and symptoms of dementia. The curator was able to confirm that people did hear footsteps and so did she. She honestly looked very relieved to know she was not going nuts and that there was actually a reason for these noises.

The Big Man
As I said before, the original owner of the house was Antonio Meucci. Amazingly enough, Meucci was actually the original inventor of the telephone. Yes, you read that right. News Alert: Alexander Graham Bell was NOT the original inventor of the telephone. The truth is that by 1857 Mr. Meucci had developed a working model of the telephone and in 1871 he was able to obtain a provisional patent from the US Patent Office. The curator went on to tell me the story of how Meucci was in a horrible ferryboat accident (could that be the boat or ship accident I was picking up on?) and had almost died. Apparently during his long recovery his wife had sold a lot of their stuff, including the plans to the telephone. Sadly, Meucci died in 1889 without ever being recognized for his invention.

The curator also confirmed that Meucci claimed Masonic membership. The Masons is a fraternal organization whose membership is held together by shared moral and metaphysical ideals. It has often been called a "secret society." Back in the day, the Masons membership list read like today's Hollywood "A" List. It included such famous people as George Washington, Harry S. Truman, Mark Twain, Henry Ford, and so on. Although she was not able to confirm Meucci's title in the Masons, we did a little research afterwards and we were able to find him listed on several Mason sites. However, we were not able to find an initiation date. I firmly believe that he was holding meetings of his own that were possibly spin-offs of the Masons. There is also a picture in the museum of Meucci and the ring he is wearing has a symbol strikingly similar to that of the Masons!

The curator also informed me that she, as well as others, has indeed seen the shadow of a man. Although at first she wasn't sure if it was Meucci or the other resident of the home named Garibaldi, but after looking at pictures of both of them I am sure it is Meucci. Their physical builds and facial features were very different, as were their energies.

The Attic
The curator and I exchanged several e-mails after the original investigation. She has since told me that she read something about Meucci's ashes having been stolen by a caretaker. They were then hidden in the rafters of the Garibaldi bedroom (which was originally the room I felt the "Big Man" Mr. Meucci in) until they were interred into the monument on the front lawn. Supposedly.

Several hours would go by as all the other teams would take their turn investigating the home. By now it was around 2:30 in the morning and we were all exhausted. At this point we were just happy to be that much closer to going home; it was time for the final walk through. This time with all the teams, we made our way through the house again one room at a time, sharing our findings and getting validation from the curator. We were almost finished as we made our way back down stairs to the main area of the house.

While I felt I had a very successful investigation, my cousin Brian, the forever skeptic, had not gotten much with any of his little gadgets, i.e. his EMF meter, digital audio recorder, and non-contact thermometer. The only thing he had gotten was some readings off a mask in a display case. That mask just happened to bc a plastcr mask, thc dcath mask of nonc othcr than Mcucci! As we stood in the main area he was discussing his findings when all of a sudden his EMF monitor started going crazy. He happened to be standing in front of a piano that Muecci had made and it seemed that the corner of the piano was omitting something. My cousin was perplexed since his earlier investigation had turned up nothing in that area. There was nothing to explain why the monitor would be going off. He followed this invisible energy into the hallway and then the monitor stopped. As we stood in the hallway chasing the "ghost," I began to feel very cold and lightheaded; the curator complained of the same symptoms. As we reentered the main area, I began to feel colder and colder. The corner of the piano continued to set the EMF monitor into frenzy and we were at a loss for an explanation. Paul (the sensitive) and I started to study the piano and we both felt that there was some sort of secret compartment. I personally did not think anything would still be in there, but it was a mystery waiting to be solved. We continued to examine the piano as much as possible but it is a museum piece and is NOT to be touched. I started being very drawn to the keys and at that exact moment Paul took off the cover and began to hit the keys. It was like a telepathic understanding as we both looked at each other. I said, "You're thinking what I am thinking." He said, "Yes." What were we thinking? We both had the same thought at the same time: the keys, when played in a specific order, would open the secret compartment. Of course having connected with Meucci earlier, I was not egotistical enough to think we could possibly figure out the code.

The EMF monitor continued going off and as we looked up we realized everyone was back over at one of the cases on the other side of the room. They were once again looking at the mask and trying to figure out a logical explanation for what could be setting it off. I began getting colder and colder and could now clearly feel someone behind me. The strange thing was that I was only cold on one side of my body! Paul also felt like something or someone was behind me. As I got colder and colder my cousin decided to see what the heck was going on. He used the non-contact thermometer to check my body temperature. To our amazement my temperature on the left side of my body was dipping down to the 70's while the right side was holding at 86 degrees. The monitor was also going off behind me on my left side. None of us, myself included, could explain what was happening, but I will tell you, it was the weirdest sensation I have ever felt. As my cousin ran the scan down my back I could feel the heat from his hand cutting through the cold chill behind me. He explained it as a gentle breeze that he could literally feel behind me.

Now I have to tell you the rest of the events are very sketchy to me. When I communicate with spirits I am totally alert and awake in appearance but I do enter some kind of different space and once I am done it is very difficult for me to recall what has taken place. In order to keep the story as accurate as possible I decided to go back to the original audio from that night. The following has been transcribed from the original tapes from that evening:

EMF monitor is going nuts...

Curator: *Do you want to tell me something? I am here everyday.*

Lisa Ann: *I swear I feel that person again and I just heard, "Yeah I want to tell you I am over here I am not over there."*

Curator: *So why are you here?*

EMF monitor goes crazy again

Brian: *Oh boy, this (the EMF monitor) is pointed at your back*

Curator: *You are right*

Lisa Ann: *I am telling you he is following me, he is right behind me on my left hand side.*

Curator: *Why are you following her?*

Paul: *Her mother is Italian isn't she?*

Brian: *My mother? Her mother?*

Lisa Ann: *My mother is Italian (of course Paul had no knowledge of that).*

Curator: *Ah that is why (Mr. Meucci is Italian, for those of you who are skipping around the story).*

Lisa Ann: *He says because I take him seriously and because I understand what it is like to feel like you have life's work to do and not just have a job, and that he wants to be taken seriously.*

Curator: *Who do you feel doesn't take you seriously?*

The monitor goes nuts and I mean nuts! We all laugh. It was either that or we all run the heck out of there!

Curator: Does this make you think that we don't take you seriously, is this why you get upset when I let certain people in?

Lisa Ann: Certain people yes.

Curator: Because I know that you get upset and I don't want you to be upset.

Lisa Ann: It is very important to him that people understand the history and what he was trying to accomplish.

Curator: That is what we try to do.

Lisa Ann: And there is a lot more that people don't know about what he has done and he says in time he will share that but he is not a very trusting person.

Curator: With good reason.

Lisa Ann: Some people that come in here come in here for their own good, not to share his story and that is what he wants, he wants people who will help him share his story.

Brian: Is there anything that we can do now to out of respect make him clear of our intentions

Lisa Ann: He would like his picture on the show and he would like a little introduction telling about who he was

Chris (the camera guy): That is standard babe, as far as what we do.

Lisa Ann: Like a little blurb.

Chris: Absolutely, we do a whole history.

Paul: Is it Garibaldi or Meucci?

Lisa Ann: Meucci, because he is the bigger guy, ya know once we came back in here and looked around the house, because when I first got here I was not allowed to look at anything but it is definitely him because the other one (Garibaldi) is thinner, he (Meucci) has a strong presence.

He is fading out. Now I am warming up a bit when the monitor goes nuts again.

Lisa Ann: He likes her (the curator) he is telling me he did not like the girl that was here before her, he is telling me he got rid of the other girl because he didn't like her. He then keeps telling me to go ahead and repeat what I am getting to the curator he says she will be able to confirm everything he is telling me. He then starts telling me about a scar he had on his right hip, he has a bad scar or something and that you know how to prove that or you know where to go to look that up (he is talking about the curator) it is on his right hip.

Brian: Could it be from the ferry accident?

Lisa Ann: I don't know, I don't feel like it is a burn, I feel like it is a cut or gash. He won't let people stay here that he doesn't like and he will do whatever it takes to get rid of them. See, I didn't feel him as an angry energy but he is very set on what he wants done and if he doesn't think someone is working for his benefit he is going to get rid of them.

Lisa Ann: He didn't like her. Do you know was there money missing? He says she was taking money. He told me she was taking money, he says that is not what this is about.

Curator: We felt she was taking money.

Lisa Ann: He says she was not a good person. She was taking money. He says those bad things; she deserved to have them happen. He says that is not what this place is about, that is not what this place is about. I think that he is the most comfortable in this room because this is where all of his stuff is. And he is telling me that the room up front he did a lot of thinking, that was his thinking room.

Curator: *The one upstairs? Yeah, he did go in there. Are you the one that sits in the chair? (She is talking to Meucci).*

Lisa Ann: *Yes, he used to like to think.*

Curator: *Sometimes people see someone sitting in that chair and someone thought they saw it earlier, my staff has seen it too recently.*

Lisa Ann: *Was there something with his stomach?*

Curator: *To my knowledge he died peacefully and of natural causes.*

Lisa Ann: *Cause I have a sharp pain in my side.*

Paul: *Back then cancer was considered natural causes.*

Curator: *Exactly, it was 1889.*

Paul: *They just didn't know.*

Lisa Ann: *He had other ideas too, that other people stole.*

Curator: *Yeah lots!*

Lisa Ann: *But he says he couldn't get them back though because part of them were part of this secret society thing, so he couldn't come out and say this is what is missing because it was secret.*

The next few minutes Meucci gave a message to Chris, the camera, guy about his brother. Chris insists the information is reversed and didn't make sense…but hey I just deliver the message. It is not my job to question the other side…

Brian: *Do you think Mr. Meucci is here all the time.*

Lisa Ann: *I think he is back and forth.   I think it is one of the places that he is drawn to but I think he has several.   I think it would be very over the top to say this is where he stays because he had a lot of places that were very meaningful to him, but this was one of them.   He is not here 24 hours a day but he definitely looks over the place.*

As I left the museum that night I couldn't help but feel that I had just had a life changing experience. I began to wonder how much of our history is really incorrect. I began to wonder how many people have not been given credit for their contributions. I also began to think about the spirits and the messages and information they have to share. I can't help but wonder how much we are really missing. In the world of information, how informed are we really?

I know that someday I will return to the museum and revisit Mr. Meucci, his wife, and all of the other spirits that still love to occupy that home. In the meantime, I feel an overwhelming obligation to Mr. Antonio Meucci and the work he did. If you would like more information on the Museum or Mr. Meucci, please visit the Museums website at:

www.community.silive.com/cc/GaribaldiMeucci

There is also a lot of information about Antonio Meucci on the web and I encourage you to look him up. I think it would be great to teach your child the correct historical facts and wouldn't it be great to teach their Social Studies teacher something new!

As a side note, I am very happy to report that in July of 2006 The Congress finally recognized Mr. Meucci as the original inventor of the telephone. I can't help but think that he is somewhere smiling down thinking, "WOW that took a long time!"   Mr. Antoino

Meucci, a pioneer and inventor, which is how he wanted to be remembered, and that is how I will always remember him.

I will continue to keep in touch with the curator of the museum as we e-mail our new theories back and forth. Who knows what else we will uncover! I file this case under "Still Opened" and I look forward to what other information Meucci will have to share.

Guidance comes when we are quiet, still, and willing to accept it.

A Teacher from the Other Side

By the time my daughter was four years old, my newfound career/life's work was in full swing. Several nights a week I would teach classes in my home. It was my nightly ritual to go into both kids' rooms to kiss them goodnight even though they were already asleep. On this one night I went into my daughter's room and noticed one of her stuffed animals on the floor. I bent down to pick it up and immediately noticed something different. Apparently the little tweedy bird stuffed animal had been clothes shopping and it was wearing a new vest. As I further investigated, it became pretty obvious that this was indeed a homemade vest. I tucked it under the covers with her and didn't think much more about it.

The next morning when she got up I went into her room and again spotted the Tweety Bird. "Did you go to grandmas last night?" I asked. "No," she said. "Well were did you get the vest for the bird from?" I asked, determined to get to the bottom of this mystery. "I made it!" she proudly exclaimed. "You made it?" I said, my curiosity now at an all time high, "Did daddy help you with it?" I continued. "No, I made it myself," she said.

I am all for supporting and encouraging your children, but seriously, how could a four-year-old make a vest for a stuffed animal? Did I mention she even had a hole cut out for Tweety's tail? Now there was no way I was letting this go. "How did you make it?" I asked. "Grandma Jennie helped me," she said without hesitation.

Now for those of you who may be skipping through this book and not reading the stories in order, Grandma Jennie is actually my Grandmother who passed away in 1991. My daughter was born in 1994 and it is now 1999. So I decided to play along. "Oh, Grandma Jennie helped you, well that is wonderful," I said. She looked at me with these big blue eyes and said, "Do you want to see how I made it?" "Of course I do!" I immediately replied. She went over to the closet and pulled out a mashed up piece of paper.

She carefully began to unfold it and then continued to spread it out onto the floor. "Grandma Jennie told me that the first thing we have to do is make a pattern," she continued. My four-year-old daughter had taken construction paper and taped four pieces together to make one big piece. Then went on to show me step by step how Grandma Jennie told her to lay the Tweety Bird down on the paper, trace around it, lay the stuffed animal on the pattern and then cut it.

I stood there with my mouth on the floor. Now I have to tell you I cannot sew so much as a button, so she did not pick this up from me. And the most shocking part of the story, for all you non-believers, is that my Grandmother was a seamstress who made the most beautiful dresses! My greatest memories of my grandmother include her incredible cooking and all of the amazing dresses she made for me throughout my life.

Later on that day, I again brought up the topic of the vest. My daughter again began to talk about her Grandma Jennie and went on and on in detail about other conversations she had been having with her.   Finally, with the innocence of a child, she looked at me and said, "Mom why is it so hard to talk to Grandma Jennie? I have to close my eyes and really listen," she said. "Can you ask God why there are no phones in heaven?"

Here is Tweety with his new vest!

The more we learn, the more we realize how little we know.

Death and Dying

I wrote this book for all of those who have lost a loved one. After reading these stories I hope you will find some sense of peace knowing that your loved ones are safe, they are around you, they watch over you, and they love you very much.

Death is not an ending but simply a transition to another place. A place filled with love and joy. In all my years of experience I have learned that there are several kinds of death. There is no perfect death. There is no death that is less painful to the one left behind. People that lose loved ones abruptly tell me how they wish they had more time to tell them how much they loved them and had a chance to say goodbye. Those who lose a loved one after a long illness tell me how they wish the person didn't have to suffer. And while each one is just as traumatizing to the person left behind, I think it is helpful to understand each type of passing.

Instant Death
This type of passing occurs either as a result of an accident or sometimes one will be diagnosed with an illness and pass almost immediately after receiving the news. Those who pass of instant death are usually those who loved life. They came here, did there work, and it was time to go home. No muss, no fuss. One minute they are here, the next they are not. They do not want to be a burden or have others taking care of them.

For those left behind, the trauma of the death and not saying good-bye is very difficult for them to deal with. But you need to understand that your loved ones are around you and can hear you. You can talk to them whenever you want and as you have seen throughout the stories in this book, they can talk to you as well.

One thing I feel is my duty to say: When people die in traumatic accidents it is very often the case that those left behind will visit the scene of the tragedy. I cannot tell you how bad this is. First of all, you need to know that your loved one is not there. They do not wish to relive that event. They are around you. More importantly, when you visit the scene, you are connecting with the psychic impression left after the accident and not your loved one. The psychic impression is a very heavy and draining feeling because of the trauma that occurred there.

I ALWAYS encourage my clients to not constantly return to the accident scene. I understand that sometimes a visit is necessary for closure but after that do not do it. Instead, remember your loved one in a positive way. Plant a garden outside your home. Set up a special spot in your home with photographs or positive memories of that person. I promise you that they will love the gesture! Most importantly, you will have a positive, relaxing place that you can go to whenever you want to be with that loved one.

Prolonged Death
This type of passing usually occurs after a long battle with a specific illness. Many times when you get the history of the person, you will find out that they have either experienced a traumatic death in their own lives, they have a fear of death, or they are worried about leaving someone behind (unfinished business so to speak). A lot of times this soul will be in and out of the body for quite sometime before actually passing. I truly believe that this is done to allow the spirit to get more comfortable with the process of passing.

This type of passing is not only hard on the person passing but on the loved ones as well. It is very important in these cases to understand that you need to constantly remind the person who is ill that you love and support them. You need to give them permission to go and assure them that everyone will be okay. This is very hard to do but it really does bring a tremendous sense of relief to the person passing. It doesn't matter if you say it out loud, it doesn't matter if the person is coherent; the spirit can always hear you.

Suicidal Death
These are the hardest readings I do. There is so much stigma attach to suicide that it is nearly impossible for the ones left behind to come to terms with the death. We are a society of judgment and

there is never more judgment than in a suicidal death. When someone loses someone to cancer it undoubtedly is a horrible loss, but there is no shame or embarrassment attached. However, when someone loses someone to suicide there is so much anger, guilt, shame, embarrassment, and stigma attached. We need to understand that suicide is many times a result of depression, and depression is an illness. Now under no circumstances do I ever feel someone should take their own life, and while I do not agree with the belief system that those who commit suicide are being punished on the other side, I will tell you that I do believe you return to repeat the same lessons over again if you end your life. Suicide is NEVER the answer. But for those who do follow through, and I have unfortunately talked to many, they are sent to a place of healing. I have NEVER had one person who committed suicide say, "I am glad I did it." They realize they did the wrong thing, but rest assured, they are not burning in proverbial Hell or reincarnating instantly to live a horrible life as punishment.

For those of you who have ever lost a loved one to suicide I have this to say to you: IT WAS NOT YOUR FAULT and THERE WAS NOTHING YOU COULD HAVE DONE DIFFERENTLY. Why do I say that? I say that because that is the most common message that comes through when I connect with those who have taken their own life. They feel horrible about how their actions have affected those they loved the most, and they assure me over and over that there was nothing anyone could have done.

For more information on suicide visit:
American Foundation for Suicide Prevention
www.afsp.org/

Helping One to Pass
Many times I am called to visit people who are terminally ill but for whatever reason they are not passing. While they are no longer here in the human sense, their bodies still remain. On those occasions, I am able to communicate with the spirit of the person who is passing to find out why they are remaining in limbo. More often than not it is one of three things: 1. They are worried about

someone they are leaving behind, 2. They are afraid that someone who has passed previously is upset with them and they are fearful of passing and seeing them again, and 3. On rare occasions the person has such a strong fear of death and is very unsure of what is on the other side. It is only by communicating with them that I can find out what the issue is and help them to find peace so they may pass.

It is very important that when you have a loved one who is in the final stages, you tell them that it is okay to go. Our human side wants them to stay but it is in that time that we need to really think about what is best for that person. And while humanly they may not be able to hear or communicate with you, I assure you the spirit is able to hear you.

A Lesson Learned
My grandfather died of colon cancer and towards the end was hardly ever in his body (meaning that his spirit was traveling back and forth to the other side). For those of you who have never been around someone who is dying, you may not understand what I mean by this. For those of you who have been around someone dying you know exactly what I mean. There are several signs when someone is in this stage. They include such things as a cold empty stare in their eyes, a hollow feeling in their body (like when you hold their hand you feel they aren't there), they may make references to seeing relatives or friends who have passed, they may talk about people that are waiting for them, and sometimes you will even feel as if they are standing next to themselves. Being a psychic and a healer I thought it would be very easy for me to help him pass and even predict when he would pass. I remember spending hours meditating on when he would pass. Towards the end, with no success, I was begging my guides and angels to tell me. I was working on him doing hands on healing (a way of using energy to reduce stress and balance the energy in the body) one day when I had a vision. I saw my grandmother who had passed years before standing in the doorway with another older woman who I did not recognize. I begged my grandmother to come in and take him. She told me that I needed to understand how the process of death and dying works. She went on to explain that while she

was allowed to be with him and let him know that she was there waiting, she was NOT allowed to come in and take him. She told me that we have free will until the moment we pass and that only we can decide when we are ready.

Later, I found out that the other woman I saw in my vision was my grandfather's mother. After telling my mother about my vision she immediately went upstairs and retrieved a photograph. To my shock, the photograph not only showed my grandmother and the unidentified woman, but they were standing exactly like I saw them in my vision. The unidentified woman was even dressed exactly how I had seen her. The only difference was my grandfather was in the photograph but not in my vision.

My grandfather's passing was such a blessing and learning experience. I was there the moment his spirit left his body and will never forget the sense of peace that overcame the room as he returned home. I knew my grandmother and greatgrandmother were right there, anxiously awaiting his arrival. I couldn't help but think that as we all stood grieving the loss of my grandfather; all of his loved ones on the other side were celebrating his arrival.

Grieving

There is a vicious cycle that happens when someone passes. Many times the person left behind does not feel the person around. Other people all around them are having dreams, visits, and encounters with the person who has passed but they are not. They immediately assume the person that has passed is upset with them in some way and that is why they are not hearing from or feeling them. That only makes the grief deepen.

You need to understand that we are energy. When we are down here on earth we vibrate at a lower vibration than when we pass. Those of us who can communicate with those who have passed are able to quite our mind and lift our vibration making it very easy for us to communicate with those on the other side. When you are grieving, it lowers your vibration and makes it nearly impossible for your loved one to get through to you.

If you have lost someone and are reading the stories in this book thinking "That never happens to me," take a step back. Know that as you work through your grief, your vibration will lift and you too will receive signs and messages from your loved ones.

A Place of Peace

Now before you all go running out booking appointments with Mediums and Psychics let me say this: Everyone on the other side is not trying frantically to get messages down here. You need to understand that when you pass you have an understanding of everyone and everything. You understand the roles that every person played in your life and why. You see how even the bad experiences with people helped you to advance and grow on a spiritual soul level. When you pass you are not holding on to all of the ridiculous things we hold onto when we are down here. Your loved ones who have passed are NOT attached to their house, their clothes, their jewelry, etc. They do not care if you move, sell their car, or change the furniture in your home. They don't care who took the money, who did what at the funeral, or who forgot to send a sympathy card. They care about one thing and one thing only: that you are happy!

Guidance from the Other Side

As I was finalizing these stories, I had a reading session that left me very disturbed and upset. I feel a very strong need to share this experience. I am hoping that even if it helps to open one person's eyes to the truth, I will have done my job.

Recently I read for a father who had lost a 17-year-old child in an auto accident. It started as a typical reading, nothing too shocking. The child came through with some very specific information that the father was able to validate, as well as messages for his mom and siblings. At the end of the reading I asked the father if he had any questions for me. He told me, as most parents do, that he just wanted to know that his child was okay. Then he looked at me with anger in his eyes and said, "Actually, I do have a question." He went on to explain that he had been raised Catholic and had been told that when family members die they watch over and protect you. He looked at me point blank and said, "I want to know what the hell my father is doing over there on the other side and how he could allow this to happen." I was shocked and speechless.

Being raised Catholic as well, I have had to reevaluate many of my beliefs about God and what I truly feel happens when we pass. I do not believe that God is a punishing God (but that is another book). I couldn't believe that this man really believed his father "allowed" his child to be killed in this car accident. I went to bed that night upset and disillusioned with what we are being told by organized religion.

Now I am no expert in anything, nor do I claim to be. My belief system comes from my personal experiences and the thousands of spirits I have communicated with, so I would like to set the record straight: We choose the experiences we have, good and bad! Yes, we chose the bad stuff too! We also choose when we are born and when we will die. I know people really struggle with this one but honestly, when it is your time to go, it is your time to go. Your loved ones are NOT allowed to interfere with your life. Yes, your loved ones are around you. Yes, they can offer guidance and support. Yes, they may even give you a heads up to things that you may wish to avoid. However, they are NOT allowed to interfere with your free will, your destiny. Bad things do not stop happening just because you have a loved one that has passed. My car accident is a perfect example of that. I did not choose that accident as a pass to the other side. I chose it as a wake up call to get my life on track. My grandmother was there to protect me to make sure I would stay here to fulfill my destiny. It was not my time to go; I had much more work to do.

You need to understand that earth is a school. Our spirits come down here simply to learn lessons and have experiences. Some times they are good and sometimes they are bad. It is a very hard concept for some people to understand, but we have chosen to have these experiences, even as horrible as some of them are.

People ask me, "Why do children die? How can that be good?" Whenever I am asked that I always think of Adam Walsh. For those of you who have no idea who that is, he is the son of John

Walsh, host of America's Most Wanted. In July 1981, Adam Walsh was murdered; he was only 6 years old. His father took that horrible tragedy and turned it into something amazing. To this day, America's Most Wanted has touched the lives of millions of people. Millions of people are safer because of that show! That is the amazing gift a little boy named Adam Walsh left behind.

Final Message
I have literally done thousands of readings connecting with people who have passed, and if I had one thing I know they would all want me to communicate to everyone reading this book it would be this:

When you lose a loved one, on your worst day I want you to remember this: If you were on the other side and your loved one was still here, wouldn't you want them to continue on with their life? You would want them to be happy and continue doing all the things they loved. That is what they want for you. They want you to be happy. They want you to honor their memory by living the happiest and most fulfilling life you can. They know that in only a short time they will be with you again. While time here is very long, time on the other side is very different.

Remember that your loved ones are always around you. Talk to them. Remember them. Honor their memory by living the happiest life you can!

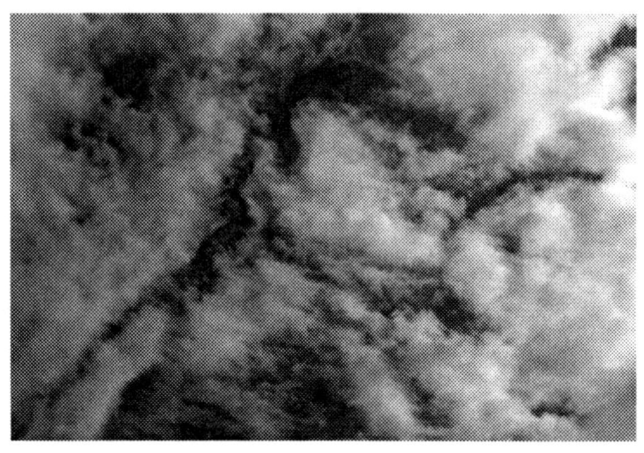

Some of us fit Spirituality into our lives, for others it becomes our life.

About Lisa Ann

Throughout my childhood I had what I call "dream visions" (I would see events in my dreams as they were actually happening). I would also get "feelings" about people and places. After I graduated high school I lost a friend to suicide. It was then that I realized the "feelings" I would get were actually energies, sometimes of people who had passed.

In my early 20's I lost my beloved grandmother, Jennie. It was at this time that my "dream visions" turned into "dream messages." My grandmother would frequently come to me in my dream state and show me things before they would happen.

Several years later, I went through a traumatic time filled with many financial and personal stresses. It was then that my journey began with a Spiritual Class that would forever change my life.

In October of 1998, my children and I were involved in a horrible car accident. The car accident strengthened my belief that I was indeed here for a reason and I felt I needed to figure out what that reason was. Three months later my grandfather was diagnosed with colon cancer. My grandfather's death was the greatest gift because it taught me the truth about life and death.

In 1996, I began doing Spiritual Readings, in 1999, I established Spiritquest Healing Center and was certified as a Reiki Master, in 2000, I was certified in Herbology, and in 2001, I was certified in Past Life Regression Training with Brain Weiss and became ordained as a Spiritual Minister.

In addition to my one-on-one sessions, I have been able to reach out to people on a larger scale through my workshops, which have included teaching at schools, libraries, and corporate organizations. My volunteer work has given me the opportunity to work with some amazing people and organizations such as Project Liberty, Hospice, nursing homes, and various mental health groups.

I continue to share my gifts and abilities with others. I am able to provide spiritual counseling through my Reading Sessions, comfort through my Medium Sessions, healing to the body, mind, and soul through my Reiki Sessions, understanding through Past Life Regression Sessions, and inner peace through my Meditation Classes and Workshops.

"Helping others to help themselves
has truly been the greatest blessing of all!"

Peace, Love, and Light,
Lisa Ann

LISA ANN

Lisa Ann is a Psychic Medium with 10 years of experience. She is able to assist clients in person or over the phone and has an international clientele. Her clients are from all walks of life, from the student who needs guidance about their future, to CEO's of companies.

Lisa Ann offers several different healing modalities and each session is structured to meet your particular needs. She also offers many different classes and workshops designed to help people take back their own power and improve their lives!

Radio
Lisa Ann has made several guest appearances on
Shannon's Corner with Shannon Devereaux Sanford (WTBQ 1110am).

Television
2005
Lisa Ann was featured in HBO Documentary "House Arrest" doing Reiki Healing.

2006
Lisa Ann was featured in "Neighborhood Journal" (Local Cablevision Channel 78) doing a Message Circle/Séance.

2007
Lisa Ann was a guest Psychic in a show called "Scared" filmed in Staten Island at the Garibaldi-Meucci Museum.

For more information on Scared visit:
www.iamhaunted.com/SCARED_TV

Books
2006
Lisa Ann was featured in "Ghost Investigator" Volume 6 by Linda Zimmermann. (Lisa Ann has accompanied Linda on several local ghost investigations.)

For more information on Linda and her work visit:
www.ghostinvestigator.com/

Guided Meditations
by Lisa Ann

*"It is only when your mind is quiet,
that your soul can be heard."*

BODY, MIND & SPIRIT HEALING CD
Body
Enjoy the amazing energy of this healing pool as you are guided through a meditation designed to put your body in perfect balance and perfect health.
Mind
Free your mind from the old belief systems and fears that hold you back. Allow the power of your mind to create a new life free of fear.
Spirit
Take a journey through the clouds as you free your spirit. Allow yourself to connect with the all-knowing spirit that lies within all of us.
Bonus
Use this short meditation to energize you for the day ahead
or to relax you for a peaceful night's sleep.

ANGELIC WHISPERS CD
White Light
Use this simple and effective exercise to prepare yourself for the day ahead or to unwind at the end of the day
Meeting Your Guides and Angels
Get in touch with your guides, angels and loved ones on this wonderful guided journey.
Chakra Balancing
Use the amazing healing energy of the Chakra system to bring balance to your body, mind and soul.
Moving Forward
Allow yourself to release the blocks from the past that keep you from moving forward in your life.

**CD's may be purchased at the on-line store, visit:
www.spiritquesthealingcenter.com**

About the Author

Lisa Ann is a Psychic, Medium, Healer, Medical Intuitive, Speaker and Teacher. She is the owner of Spiritquest Healing Center and Spiritquest Productions. She is available for private sessions, lectures, seminars, and book signings.

If you would like to contact her:

Write to:

Spiritquest
P.O. Box 174
Slate Hill, NY 10973

Email:

lisaann@spiritquesthealingcenter.com

For more information

on Lisa Ann, Spiritquest Healing Center or
Spiritquest Productions go to:
www.spiritquesthealingcenter.com

I hope this book has brought you peace, strength, and understanding.

Peace, Love, and Light
Lisa Ann

Printed in the United States
78273LV00002B/1-99